The Night Jamie Lost Her Shit

by Jamie L. Miller

Copyright © 2020 Jamie L. Miller

All rights reserved. This book or any portion thereof may not be reproduced or used in any manner whatsoever without the express written permission from the publisher, except for the use of brief quotations in a book review.

ISBN 978-1-71660-731-8

Characters and events in this book are NOT fictitious. Any similarity to real persons, living or dead, is NOT coincidental and IS intended by the author.

Printed and bound in the U.S.A.

First Edition September 2020

This book is dedicated to all of
you who have lost your own shit
on at least one occasion!

A loving husband.

Two amazing daughters.

A nice home in a quiet neighborhood.

A rewarding job.

And a really cool car.

It was Winter.

Jamie started hearing chatter about a new virus that had entered the country.

Chatter quickly turned into obsession.

COVID-19 suddenly became the main topic of conversation everywhere.

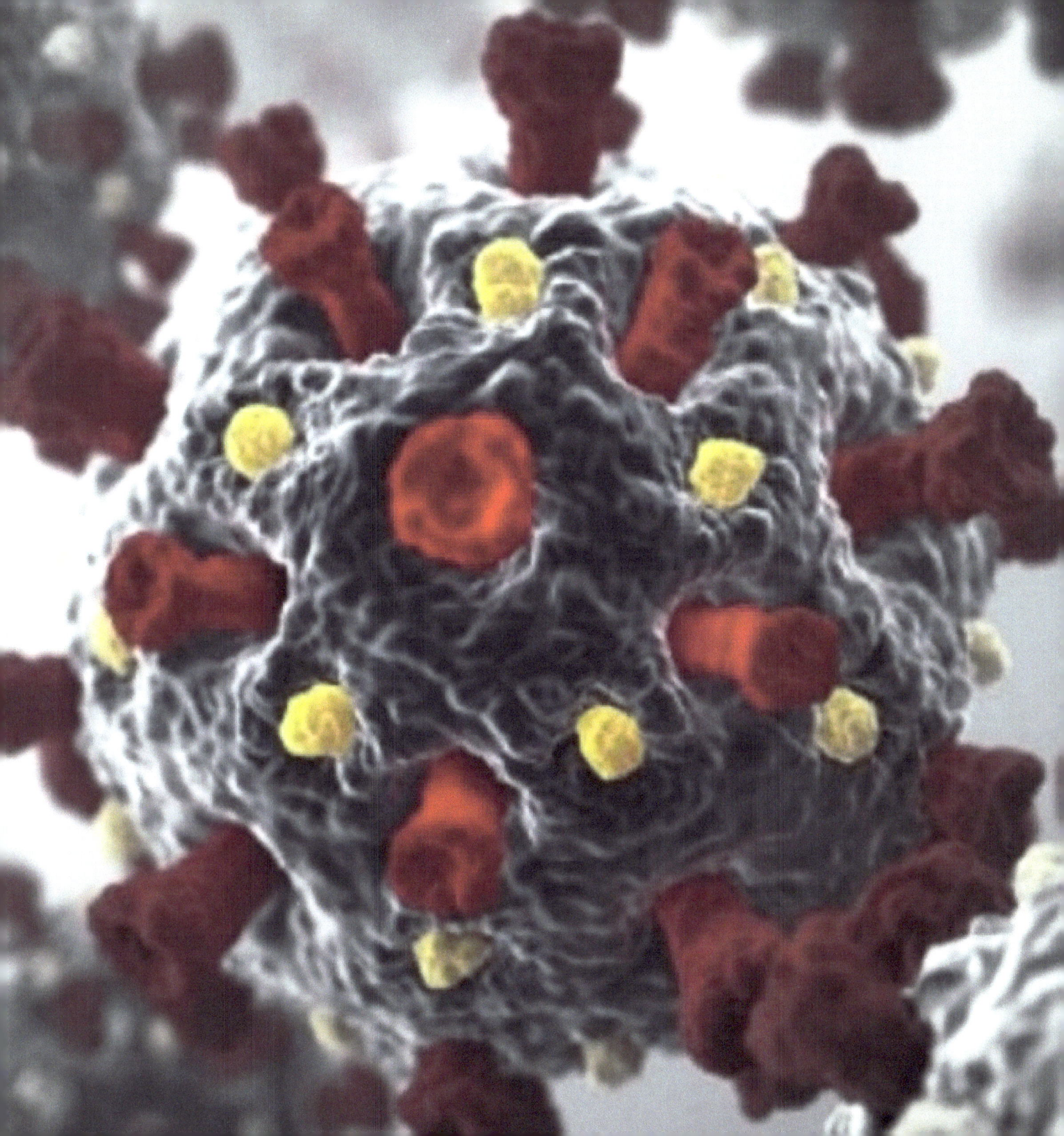

Days passed.

The virus continued to spread.

The chatter grew louder.

People around the world were dying.

Fear became real.

The state had to respond.

March 13, 2020

Pennsylvania schools were abruptly shut down for the next 14 days.

In only a few short weeks...

All restaurants and "non-essential" businesses were ordered to close their doors.

It was nearly impossible to find toilet paper at the grocery store.

School closures across the state were extended for an "indefinite period of time."

A "stay at home" ordinance was issued.

Jamie could no longer go to work.

Her kids could no longer go to school.

They didn't leave the house.

Jamie read the news every day.

Over and over again.

Doom and negativity oozed from every updated report.

Confusion and fear grew.

Jamie felt like she was in constant waiting for the next bit of bad news.

It was like watching the weather radar and waiting for the storm to hit.

Jamie's husband continued to go to work every day.

He didn't obsess over the news.

He didn't feel the fear of the unknown.

He continued to have daily social interactions outside of the house.

April 3, 2020

The governor announced that everyone must wear a mask when not in their own homes.

Yes, it was a safety measure.

It was also a grave reminder of how serious this unknown illness was.

For Jamie, it was the icing on the cake.

The straw that broke the camel's back.

Jamie felt like she was suffocating.

Drowning.

Gasping for air.

Jamie needed to get away.

She needed to get outside and feel the night air fill her lungs.

But her husband didn't want to go for a walk.

Jamie's husband didn't understand why she was so upset.

It wasn't his fault though.

He couldn't understand why.

His everyday life hadn't really changed.

Jamie knew she needed to get outside!

So she ventured into the dark of the night on her own.

She began to walk a familiar path.

As she walked, tears mixed with the cold rain that stung her face.

With each step, Jamie walked faster and faster.

She cried harder and harder.

The world appeared to be

blurry

and

muted.

Jamie felt alone.

Confused.

Hopeless.

Above all, Jamie felt angry.

So angry.

Angry at the world for turning upside down and inside out.

Angry that she couldn't understand or know what would happen next.

Jamie trekked from one stop sign to the next.

Hot tears streaked her flushed cheeks.

Then a porch light came into sight.

A few friends from the neighborhood waved to Jamie from the porch.

They shouted "Hello!" and "How are you?"

Jamie waved back,
but could not find a positive voice.

With a sob, Jamie finally managed to sputter,

And she did just that.

Jamie walked.

Jamie cried.

She counted forward to 20.

She counted backward from 20.

Then did it all again.

After a few blocks, the rain no longer stung as it landed on her cheeks.

Jamie started to notice the little things around her.

The "For Sale" sign on an old Victorian home.

The "Hoo, Hoo, Hooooo" of an owl in the distance.

Jamie walked a little slower.

Tears no longer streamed from her eyes.

She felt each breath come easier and steadier.

The air felt a little lighter.

Jamie found herself back at the house where a few neighborhood friends had gathered.

They welcomed her to join them.

Jamie sat on the bottom stair of the porch.

Each one of them kept a respectable distance from the others.

Jamie told them how she was feeling.

Angry.   Anxious.

Sad.   Lonely.

Unsure.   Afraid.

It turned out that she wasn't alone.

Each person on that porch had feelings of worry, too.

Worry for themselves.

Worry for their family members.

Worry for their jobs and financial security.

No one knew what to expect next.

It was a grim truth.

But it also brought an honest realization...

NONE OF THEM WERE ALONE.

They would move forward together.

One step at a time.

One foot in front of the other.

For that one hour of the night, Jamie finally felt like she could breathe again.

She knew that she wasn't going to drown.

She could accept that things might get worse before they got better.

But now Jamie knew she didn't have to swim the murky waters on her own.

Jamie went home feeling like she could keep breathing.

One breath at a time.

One day at a time.

Maybe even when wearing a mask.

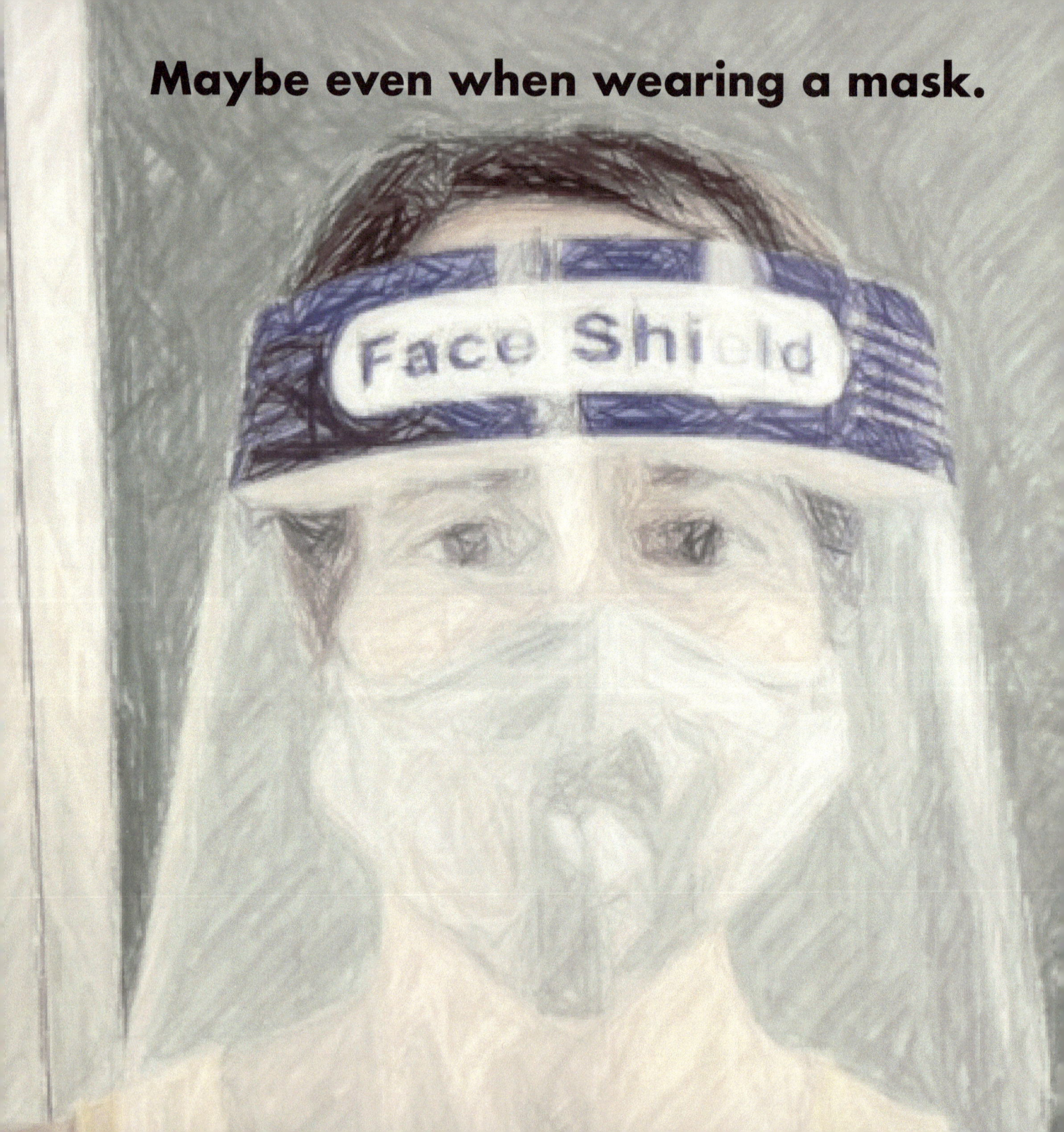

Crisis Text Line
(24/7, anonymous, free crisis counseling)
Text SIGNS to 741741

OK2Talk Teen Helpline
1-800- 273-TALK

Substance Abuse & Mental Health Services Administration (SAMSHA) National Helpline
1-800-662-HELP (4357)

Suicide Prevention Lifeline
1-800-273-8255

Veterans Crisis Line
1-800-273-8255

www.ingramcontent.com/pod-product-compliance
Lightning Source LLC
LaVergne TN
LVHW072054070426
835508LV00002B/94